IL FARO
CAPO FERRO
LIGHTHOUSE

PORTO CERVO MARINA
YACHT CLUB COSTA SMERALDA

HOTEL PITRIZZA

CERVO HOTEL

MONTI di MOLA

PEVERO GOLF CLUB

PEVERO HEALTH TRAIL

HOTEL ROMAZZINO

CALA di VOLPE

SPIAGGIA del PRINCIPE
SPIAGGIA POLTU DI LI COGGHI

LISCIA RUJA

NIKKI BEACH COSTA SMERALDA

PORTISCO

COSTA
SMERALDA

Text by Cesare Cunaccia

COSTA
SMERALDA

ASSOULINE

INTRODUCTION

Perched on a rugged stretch of coastline punctuated by pink granite rocks, Costa Smeralda overlooks the sparkling Tyrrhenian Sea in northeastern Sardinia. This exclusive destination is gently tucked away among the beaches of Rena Bianca, Liscia di Vacca and Pitrizza. Until the early 1960s, the area was difficult to access by land, hemmed in by steep bluffs covered with woods and knotted scrub. To reach the sea, visitors had to fight their way down through a tangle of tenacious mastic trees and thorny junipers, on a descent made even more arduous by rocky conformations barbed like ramparts. Along the coast, there were no human settlements—and no roads—within this prehistoric and pristine natural environment. Ahead of you, there was only a shimmering surface of clear waters in a palette of sapphire, turquoise, tourmaline, peridot and emerald, glistening with a thousand and one reflections.

In its sixty years of existence, Costa Smeralda has become one of the most mythical places in the Mediterranean. Its founder, Prince Karim Aga Khan, had an extraordinary intuition about the place, built on Sardinia's unique characteristics: the environment, culture and traditions of an ancient island that had yet to be discovered by international tourism. More than simply a wonderful place, Costa Smeralda is a registered trademark and a private tourist destination. It is an unprecedented invention that embodies a concept of tourism and belonging based on a visionary gamble that today appears in many ways prescient. Costa Smeralda represents a design achievement that has changed the notion of hospitality around the world. The location itself

Ringo Starr arrives in Costa Smeralda, 1960s.
Previous pages: Cala Petra Ruja Beach in Costa Smeralda, in the region of Sardinia known as Gallura.
Pages 4–5: The granite rock that welcomes visitors to Costa Smeralda in Sardinia, Italy.

is hard to ignore, starting with its dazzling, almost prodigious beginnings. Along with its distinctive architecture, beaches and glamorous icons, it has always retained an understated elegance and maintained an intimate dialogue with nature.

To capture the harmony between nature and the spontaneous forms found within a primordial landscape, the Aga Khan commissioned the leading architects of the day to create a distinct architectural style to represent Costa Smeralda. Borrowing elements from other Mediterranean countries such as Spain, Morocco, Tunisia and Greece, the design aesthetic blended harmoniously into the wild Sardinian landscape, with its extensive woodlands and large quantities of stone. In the beginning it was an enclave nestled in a primitive setting that welcomed the world's elite with great simplicity. In this other dimension, international visitors found what they were looking for: a place with unbridled potential and great silences in an exclusive, unattainable reality. Haute couture outfits alternated with denim shorts and tattered hippie T-shirts, fabulous jewelry worn with vintage clothing, voluminous caftans, nude hues and tousled, highlighted hair. The Costa Smeralda mythology consists of an incomparable natural beauty miraculously preserved in its original state, and an exclusive set of legendary (and eccentric) visitors—such as the photographer Lord Patrick Lichfield, cousin of Queen Elizabeth II— who helped define the story of Costa Smeralda, and above all a crystal-clear sea of infinite colors. The gods here lived hidden away, entrenched behind enclosures that were insurmountable for most people and that required a password. A fantasy fiction of beaches and coves of almost tropical white sand permeated with light, lunar rocks sculpted by the wind, sports competitions, beauty, privilege and glamour. There are special places with unusual destinies, predetermined by their DNA to occupy an extraordinary, unique dimension. Costa Smeralda belongs to this category of exceptional destinations.

The Sardinians were afraid of the sea—its pirates and invaders—especially in the Dark Ages, so they settled away from the coasts, camouflaging the *stazzi* (farmhouses) and the enclosures of goats and sheep in the rough landscape, fearing raids and incursions. The nearby town of Arzachena and the surrounding area have been inhabited for millennia. There are remains of Neolithic civilizations dating back some five thousand years, such as the necropolis of Li Muri, the only ancient, circular cemetery in Sardinia and the oldest in the entire territory. The village and the Nuraghe La Prisgiona were built in the Nuragic period, spanning from the fourteenth century BCE to the eighth century BCE, while the mysterious Tombs of the Giants date to the Bronze Age (around 1800 BCE). In more recent times, the village of Arzachena grew around the Church of Santa Maria, whose exterior is engraved with the date 1776.

It was in the 1950s that the first yachts were sighted along the coast, at the same time that Milanese Giuseppe "Kerry" Mentasti purchased the isle of Mortorio, and then a few years later, he bought the land and the bay of Porto Cervo to make it a fishing and hunting reserve. Costa Smeralda garnered additional attention in 1959 after a visit from John Duncan Miller, who was the European representative for the International Bank for Reconstruction and Development, part of the World Bank. Having returned to London after overseeing work financed with World Bank loans, Miller went back to Sardinia and was guided around Monti di Mola (as the area was known at the time) by a regional politician, the honorable Giovanni Filigheddu. Miller fell in love with the place's archaic beauty and authentic landscapes, and spoke of its allure to friends and acquaintances, including the forty-ninth Imam of the Ismailis, Prince Karim Aga Khan. Just a few years later, on March 14, 1962, the twenty-five-year-old prince and the other founding

Previous pages: Diving off the coast of Passo delle Galere.
Following pages: Prince Karim Aga Khan, architect Luigi Vietti, Paolo Riccardi and others survey a location overlooking the bay in what would become Porto Cervo.

partners—lawyer André Ardoin, Felix Bigio, the prince's half-brother Patrick Benjamin Guinness, René Podbielski and John Duncan Miller—signed the deed of incorporation of the Consorzio Costa Smeralda, which gave life to the extraordinary entity that would become Costa Smeralda.

It was on a hot summer night in 1962 that an agreement was reached between the Mentasti family and Prince Aga Khan on the sale of the one hundred hectares at the center of Porto Cervo, the beating heart of Costa Smeralda. The consortium was set up to manage the project. In autumn 1963, the Aga Khan, architect Luigi Vietti, Paolo Riccardi and other professionals found a place high on the hill overlooking the bay and referred to as Isula di Unfarru, or Inferno. Below them was a crystalline sea and a steep, craggy terrain marked only by goat tracks. "Next year, on August 14, Porto Cervo will be here," declared Prince Karim. An organization like no other in the Mediterranean region, the consortium followed every detail of the construction process, solved problems and became an irreplaceable reference point for everyone involved in the Costa Smeralda venture, both then and now.

The Aga Khan was the undisputed protagonist in the establishment of this incredible union between environment and architecture. A pioneer in sustainability in its broadest sense, he first came to Sardinia in 1960. In 1961 he disembarked in Olbia to visit an area near Arzachena: Monti di Mola, or "Millstone Hills," since the local stone was used to make millstones for grinding wheat. During his visit he was accompanied by lawyer André Ardoin, who was the legal historian for the Aga Khan's family and provided crucial support to the prince throughout his Sardinian chronicle. At the time, the area was completely isolated, with no roads, electricity or running water.

Hotel Cala di Volpe, illustration by Josh McKenna.

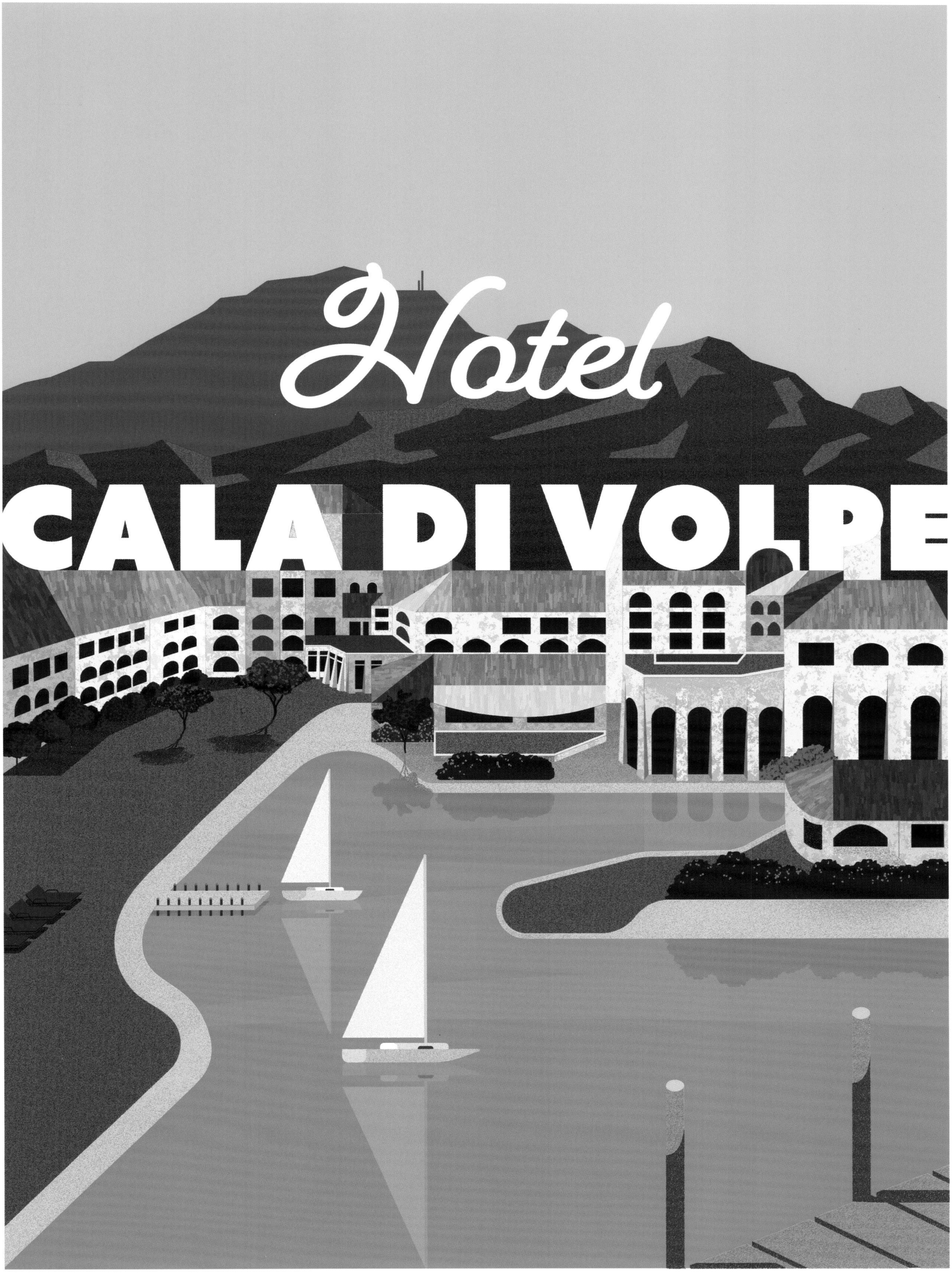
Hotel
CALA DI VOLPE

There was nothing there; it was like being on the moon. It was Ardoin who had the idea to create a major tourist development, having been seduced by the breathtaking, unspoiled beaches. This is how the ambitious project began its life, with the acquisition of large parcels of land, supported by John Duncan Miller, who had been one of the first to discover the location.

Young and charismatic, the Aga Khan, who mastered Italian in just a couple of years (his paternal grandmother was Italian, and his father, Aly, was born in Turin), was the engine of the dream he pursued. He supervised every detail with meticulous attention, hiring exceptional consultants and architects as part of a futuristic intervention designed with the utmost respect for the ecosystem. He was a real estate entrepreneur who launched himself into an investment program spread over fifty years. This is how Costa Smeralda, a development unique in Italy and perhaps the entire world, came into being. It was accompanied by a host of myths and legends, including the origin of its name, attributed to Giuseppe Mentasti. His suggestion, Costa Esmeralda, after his daughter, was revised by architect Luigi Vietti, who removed the initial "E" with the approval of the Aga Khan and his investors. Other theories on the origins of the name, which are not so far-fetched, relate to the color of the water, which in many areas takes on an emerald tone.

The founding concept of Costa Smeralda is based on the idea of a sustainable tourist development and an intense dialogue with the natural environment. It is a treasure to be safeguarded with love and respect, entrusted to protective hands according to the vision of its founder: Prince Karim Aga Khan (or "K," as he was known), who succeeded his grandfather Aga Khan III in 1957 to become leader of the Ismaili Muslims. Costa Smeralda's sublime natural landscape, which was preserved thanks to its long period of isolation, is what gives the place its allure. And the sea, an indescribable sea.

Another of its aristocratic admirers, Prince Carlo Giovanelli, who fell in love with Costa Smeralda in 1965, observed that the most profound meaning of the location—its authentic soul—was in its inextricable relationship with the sea. There is a delicate balance between the natural environment and urban development, particularly with a focus on tourism. If it is not carefully managed, development can cause damage in ecologically sensitive zones, create elevated consumption of natural resources and increase pollution. The Consorzio Costa Smeralda continues to monitor its performance in sustainable practices and implement improvements, ensuring the proper function and protection of its tourist entity.

During the 1980s, the prince ceded control of the Consorzio Costa Smeralda to international groups until the arrival of Qatar, which, with its subsidiary Smeralda Holding, redesigned the future of Costa Smeralda to regain its position of prominence among luxury tourist destinations. Today the consortium is made up of more than 3,800 owners of land, houses and tourist activities, and only those associated with the Consorzio Costa Smeralda can claim the coveted Costa Smeralda address.

In the early 1960s, an influential architecture committee was formed under the presidency of Prince Karim, with architects Jacques Couëlle, Raymond Martin, Michele Busiri-Vici, Luigi Vietti and Antonio Simon Mossa. The buildings were first simulated on-site with models made of wooden poles, so the team could assess the impact on the landscape. It was an avant-garde vision at the time and reveals how well these professionals—who, apparently, often disagreed vehemently and were capable of poisonous criticism—had understood the paramount importance of designing with the utmost respect for the environment. Hotel Cala di Volpe was designed by Jacques Couëlle in

Following pages: (*left*) Marisa Berenson in Costa Smeralda, photographed by Henry Clarke for *Vogue*, 1969. (*right*) Architectural detail at Cervo Hotel.

1961 and later modified by his son Savin, who lived mainly in Costa Smeralda. The building's sinuous curves follow the coastline, extending out to the sea via the dock and elongated jetty. It was inspired by the archaic architectural style of the local buildings: a dialogue between stone (granite) and wood featuring a rhythmic pattern of staggered floors and roofs, arcades, expertly aged plaster, dreamlike turrets and fireplaces. Couëlle, who was a friend of Dalí and Picasso, liked to describe himself as an architect-sculptor, and his villa at Monti Mannu looked like an amazing organic sculpture, a fantastic brutalist animal derived from a menhir suspended in time, as coarse and rough as a rock. Couëlle molded model sculptures on iron wire frames, which were then made to scale, creating sculptural houses without right angles, whose forms were terse and primal yet as soft and welcoming as a hug.

The great Luigi Vietti, the architect and urban planner who had previously produced the master plan for Cortina d'Ampezzo and Portofino, was responsible for the village of Porto Cervo, Cervo Hotel and the magnificent Hotel Pitrizza, a sustainable telluric construction camouflaged to integrate it into the landscape. The hotel's single-story villas, made with local materials and practically covered in greenery, blend perfectly into the Mediterranean scrub that descends to the beach. Everything Vietti created was organic and rational. He also designed the Dolce Sposa complex and various villas—such as the Cerbiatte, which Prince Karim chose as his residence, and the Romazzine, on the promontory of the same name—along with the complexes of Cala Granu and Cala del Faro. During the design process of Costa Smeralda, Vietti collaborated closely with the ceramics manufacturer Cerasarda, which reinvented local Sardinian styles with vivid Mediterranean colors, a typical feature of many Costa Smeralda interiors. Vietti also owned a classic sailboat, *Tamory,* and was one of the founders of the Yacht Club Costa Smeralda.

Michele Busiri-Vici, whom everyone remembers as a lovely, helpful person, was the descendant of generations of Roman architects and aristocrats. He designed Hotel Romazzino (1965), Sa Conca condominium, Hotel Luci di la Muntagna and the church of Stella Maris (1966), a sacred building enriched with gates and furnishings by Luciano Minguzzi and a *Mater Dolorosa* above the altar by Doménikos Theotokópoulos (El Greco), donated by a refined woman of faith. Busiri-Vici's Sardinian architecture is permeated with a powerful sculptural quality and uses locally sourced materials, contrasted by dazzling white lime plasterwork.

These pioneers, who developed a distinctive, sustainable style of architecture that tried, at all costs, to protect the incomparable natural surroundings, were eventually followed by other architects and designers active in the nearby towns. They included Savin Couëlle, Peter Schneck, Jean Paul De Marchi, Giuseppe Polese, Gerard Béthoux, Gianni Gamondi and Enzo Satta. All contributed, in their own way, to a building philosophy well ahead of its time, interweaving organic forms, rationalism, dreamlike elements and contemporary idioms. The buildings blend in, assimilating themselves into ridges and hillsides, trying to make as little impact as possible on the integrity of the land they stand on. They are harmonious extensions, tonal chords rather than jarring intrusions on the pristine Mediterranean environment.

In line with the extremely high standards of quality and professionalism that have always set Costa Smeralda apart, the renovation team includes world-renowned architects such as Dordoni Architects, Bruno Moinard and Matteo Thun.

Following pages: The early years of Porto Cervo.

In Costa Smeralda, yesterday's rituals have evolved into today's, as the destination continues to be a crossroads for the elite. Aperitifs start at seven at Cala di Volpe, a time-honored tradition, with many arriving by boat. The crowd is eclectic and international. You can have lunch at the classic Cala Barbecue, where the same guests come year after year, or at Novikov, preferred by the younger generation. Matsuhisa at Cala di Volpe serves Japanese and fusion cuisine in a wonderful setting. The Beefbar, also at Cala, is a concept restaurant created by Riccardo Giraudi in Monte Carlo over a decade ago. When the sun goes down, young people head over to Phi Beach, an atmospheric club, bar and restaurant where you can dance the night away among the rocks to the beats of international DJs. Meanwhile, the ideal place for a romantic dinner for two is the terrace of Hotel Pitrizza, preceded by cocktails at sunset. The nightclub scene is dominated by Sottovento, the legendary Ritual club (launched in 1970 and carved into the rock) and Billionaire, owned by Flavio Briatore, who also opened the restaurant Assunta Madre. The thrilling regattas organized by the local yacht club attract a cosmopolitan crowd, the highlights being the Rolex Cup, Wally Cup and Veteran Boat Rally, a race dedicated to vintage boats. The epicenter of these sailing events, which take place from April to September, is the Yacht Club Costa Smeralda, with its stunning staircase, its suites for members and a magnificent swimming pool where you can enjoy a delightful breakfast. The new urban area of the Promenade is also very popular, with its blend of high-end boutiques and art galleries.

The real protagonists of Costa Smeralda's social life have traditionally shied away from the spotlight. In the 1960s, when Prince Karim was engaged to the Begum Salimah, her privacy was heavily guarded: Paparazzi were banned or thrown out of this paradise by tenacious security guards, who were hard

Ferrari 857S Scaglietti on display at Poltu Quatu Classic 2020.

to evade. "The best thing about Costa Smeralda is the mix of Old World and New World," a veteran confides. "The pristine nature and amazing sea, astonishing boats and villas, tropical sand and rocks like sculptures shaped by the wind. There are legends and gossip, amplified by the media, but ultimately the true story of Costa Smeralda takes place away from prying eyes, and everything remains protected by an impenetrable screen of confidentiality. Entertainment is guaranteed for all ages and tastes. Here, even if you are a celebrity, you can enjoy the simple pleasure of walking barefoot along a beach, in contact with nature."

Hotel Romazzino is the perfect place to spend a lazy day under an umbrella on the beach, or for the more active, there is waterskiing. Enjoy lunch on the dazzling shore at Nikki Beach or at White on Long Beach. The iconic Rosemary restaurant has been taken over and revamped by Pacifico and features a live DJ. For something a little different, there's the market at San Pantaleo, the latest stylish boho haunt, just a short distance from Costa Smeralda. Giagoni restaurant in Piazzetta is very picturesque. Seafood lovers flock to Quattro Passi al Pescatore, Porto Cervo's first restaurant. Designed by Jacques Couëlle in the 1960s and built on the Vecchio Molo, it recently underwent a complete renovation, and is now led by chef Antonio Mellino, who was awarded two Michelin stars for his other restaurant, Quattro Passi, in Nerano. The view of the marina is unbeatable, managed by IGY Marinas, which has set the benchmark for luxury and quality in nautical tourism around the world.

Fashion has been a major contributor to the colorful narrative of Costa Smeralda, starting with Bettina Graziani in the 1950s, the muse of Jacques Fath and then a model for Dior, Grès and Balmain. Graziani graced the covers of the world's top magazines and helped organize Hubert de Givenchy's first fashion show in 1952. She was also the longtime companion of Prince Aly Khan after his divorce from Rita Hayworth. Costa Smeralda has attracted many sophisticated women, such as Dolores Guinness, a heraldic beauty who dominated the pages of *Vogue, Town & Country* and *Harper's Bazaar* in outfits by Balenciaga, Dior and Yves Saint Laurent. She was captured on film by the best photographers in the world, including Bert Stern, Slim Aarons, Cecil Beaton, Richard Avedon and William Klein. Then there was Marisa Berenson, a model and actress of patrician beauty who was the granddaughter of Parisian surrealist designer Elsa Schiaparelli. She was immortalized by Henry Clarke and Nello di Salvo in numerous famous shoots of the late 1960s, exuding a sidereal, aristocratic allure, with the eyes of a Spanish infanta or a Palmyrene goddess in robes. Couturiers loved her, especially Pucci, Valentino—whom she helped launch internationally—and Irene Galitzine, the charming Russian princess who invented the palazzo pajama, an indispensable fashion item in the 1960s and '70s. Berenson later turned to acting, but remains a global fashion icon to this day. She still remembers arriving in Costa Smeralda as a young woman, just a few years after it was created, a natural paradise far removed from reality.

In a shot by Slim Aarons, Donna Barbara Selvaggia Borromeo moves through the water like a contemporary naiad against a limpid tourmaline backdrop. Some of the first visitors to Costa Smeralda included Valentino and Giancarlo Giammetti, Mariuccia Mandelli of Krizia (who had close ties with Sardinia), Ottavio and Rosita Missoni, Gianni Versace and Giorgio Armani—Italy's fashion royalty. Another couple inextricably linked with the area, particularly between the 1980s and the early 2000s, are Roberto and Eva Cavalli, whose creative vision of boho glamour characterized by animal prints and a sexy, libertarian wilderness aesthetic—windswept hair,

Following pages: Sunbather at Hotel Cala di Volpe, 1967, photographed by Slim Aarons.

barbarian jewelry, bandannas and sheer fabrics—created the perfect mood for Costa Smeralda. A constant presence in Costa Smeralda, Roberto and Eva Cavalli spent entire summers partying there, in their zebra-striped dinghy loaded with superb women and on the yacht with an iridescent hull. The world's top supermodels followed Cavalli: Naomi Campbell, who for whole seasons would feature prominently in the gossip columns, along with Cindy Crawford, Claudia Schiffer and Eva Herzigova. And this lineup wouldn't be complete without Sardinian designer Antonio Marras, from the Catalan enclave of Alghero. A true poet with a limitless imagination, he often drew inspiration from the folklore and ancestral culture of his land, mixing them with literary and artistic references from every age and origin.

The promontory of Capo Ferro rises from the sea between Liscia di Vacca and Porto Cervo, dominated by a lighthouse high among the reddish-brown rocks. Behind lies Cala Granu, a white sandy beach that could be in the Caribbean. When the mistral blows, especially in autumn, venturing out here is a unique experience. The powerful wind is shocking with its salty, violent howl steeped in Mediterranean echoes and evocations, conveyor of ancestral sagas and customs and the legacies of the Gallura shepherds. It seems to break free of the Earth itself and fly away. Liscia Ruja, on the provincial road between Olbia and Porto Cervo, is accessible via a busy dirt road. The beach, which is just over a third of a mile long, is a paradise of white sand that turns to pink, bordered by a scrub of strawberry trees and rock roses. Poltu Li Cogghi is about five miles from Porto Cervo. Even today, the enclave gives you an idea of what Costa Smeralda must have been like before its modern discovery. Time stands still as you gaze at the glittering sand, dappled with scrub in shades of green from which amazing granite forms emerge. Many people know it as the "Spiaggia del Principe"— the Beach of the Prince—and it can be reached only by foot, taking the road that leads to Hotel Romazzino. Mortorio, an island of just over a third of a square mile, is only a few minutes' boat ride off Costa Smeralda. With the islet of Soffi and the rock of Mortoriotto, it forms a small archipelago facing Porto Cervo. Boats can land at Cala Occidentale, a bay of shimmering waters in an incredible palette of greens and blues, and at Cala Orientale, protected by a cloister of rose-pink granite that ensures the sea within is calm even in the event of the most furious mistral.

Limestone cliffs soaring into the blue alternate with silver-flecked sand dunes and pink granite rocks with bizarre or rounded shapes, like gigantic shells sculpted by the powerful salty wind. The coastline is carved by fjords created by the gradual advance of the sea in the ancient river valleys that the Sardinians call *"rias,"* recalling the Spanish dominion. The *"macchia Mediterranea"*—Mediterranean scrub—of wild olives, carob trees, mastics, laurels, myrtles, rock roses, junipers and strawberry trees fades into an alchemy of sage, heather, thyme, rosemary and broom redolent of spicy, aromatic scents, lashed by the vital energy of the salty marine air. At the first rays of sunshine in spring, sinuous orchids appear as if by magic on the quartzite beach, flaunting unusual colors that seem almost unreal. This is the Big Blue. Because Costa Smeralda doesn't belong to anyone—it is she who owns you.

“I believe that Sardinia is a magical, very powerful land.”

Caterina Murino, *actress*

“ At times I cannot find the words to describe what I see and perceive when I explore my land. It is the multifaceted face of an island whose every corner is so different and fascinating that you instantly establish contact with its most remote nature. ”

Marcello Chiodino, *photographer*

66 Here on the Costa Smeralda I admired the millennial olive tree in Luras, given Natural Monument status, and then, for the first time, a nuraghe. I was struck by how imposing these great structures are, and by this lost civilization which left behind such impressive testimonies. 99

Piero Angela, *journalist and pianist*

" They are my favorite moments of the day when I am in Costa Smeralda. I have a swim as soon as I wake up in the morning, every day, weather permitting, and then, in the evening at sunset, I sit at home and watch the Pevero bay as it changes colors, the boats as they glide by, the birds flying, the light fading. Nature is wonderful. I feel it and I need it. "

Guglielmo Miani, *CEO of Larusmiani*

66 I can't help but love Sardinia.... I came here for the first time many years ago. I arrived by boat. And, if there is one thing I haven't forgotten, it is the emerald green of the sea. I remember thinking that there never was a more perfect name for a place. **99**

Giorgio Armani, *designer*

" I came to Sardinia for the first time about twenty years ago, and since then, I've come here every year. I love everything about it: the sea, coast, rocks, plants, people, food, architecture and its distinctive peace and quiet. "

Arkady Novikov, *restaurateur*

66 My father loved this island, and he brought us here when we were just kids. At first, we would come a couple of weekends every year for the regattas, then gradually more and more often, for longer and longer. I have so many memories of those incredible holidays. The hours flew by, from the first morning dip in the sea to the last swim at night. 99

Vittoria Loro Piana

66 Sardinia is a wonderful place inhabited by wonderful people. Not to mention the food and wine. We arrived in winter and left in summer. We loved every single minute of this experience, and we made great friendships that will stay in our hearts forever. Italy is my second home. 99

George Clooney, *actor*

" We always leave Sardinia sad in our hearts because we truly desire to stay longer. We have the dream of one day retiring in Costa Smeralda, or at least spending half of the year in our special, magical Mediterranean land. We have traveled many places over the years, but we have to admit that there is no place like our Sardinian *casa*. "

Paige Adams-Geller, *co-founder and creative director of Paige*

"Transparency is what I look for most. Ideally, I'd like my houses to disappear altogether into the landscape so that my clients can enjoy such a direct contact with nature that they forget about everything else."

Savin Couëlle, *architect*

"Paradise seekers landed here, betraying the legendary Mediterranean queens from Saint-Tropez to Sorrento, from Capri to Portofino."

Lina Wertmüller, *film director*

"It's a place that has managed to maintain its extraordinary beauty while making itself the envy of the world, in terms of the top leisure opportunities on offer. Today it's one of the places that best unite the creed of environmental sustainability with a sense of health and well-being."

Alfonso Dolce, *CEO of Dolce&Gabbana*

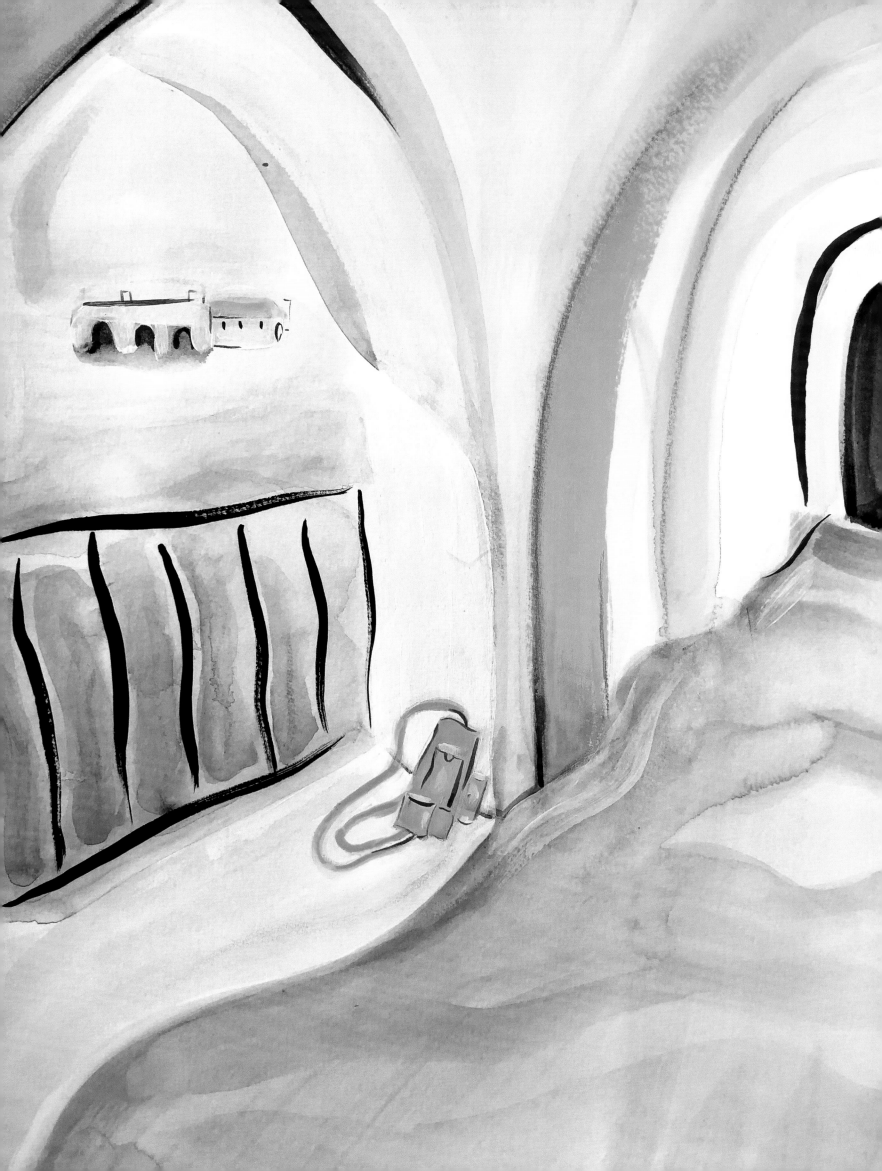

"I've been to many places around the world, truly enchanting places, but none of them hold a candle to Sardinia and, in particular, this hotel."

Princess Giulia De Gregorio Cattaneo di Sant'Elia

66 This land does not resemble any other place. Sardinia is another thing: larger, much more than usual, not at all irregular, but that disappears in the distance. Enchanting space and distance to travel around, nothing done, nothing definitive. It's like freedom itself. **99**

D. H. Lawrence, *writer*

66 The sea here takes on particularly lovely hues ranging from the darkest blue to the purest green. There are scores of fine, sandy beaches…. Rugged green and grey mountains drop abruptly toward the water. A carpet of purple and yellow, and red and blue flowers perfumes the air. 99

Prince Karim Aga Khan

"Another reason why Sardinia is unique: It is a perfectly balanced mix between confidentiality and exhibitionism, class and bohemianism, etiquette and extravagance, extreme luxury and simplicity."

Francesca Lombardi, *writer*

CAPTIONS

Monoskiing in the bay by Hotel Cala di Volpe.

Rooftop terrace of the Harrods Suite at Hotel Cala di Volpe.

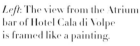

Left: The view from the Atrium bar of Hotel Cala di Volpe is framed like a painting.

Right: *Flying Dragon*, owned by Paolo Scerni, at the Maxi Yacht Rolex Cup 2006, Porto Cervo.

The Old Port as seen from the Piazzetta in Porto Cervo, 1960s.

Left: (From left) Donna Ines Torlonia, Donna Marina Lante della Rovere, Donna Paola Punturieri and Conte Dino Pecci Blunt on the bow of *Gitana III*.

Right: Princess Margaret, Countess of Snowdon, and her friend on the Aga Khan's yacht, 1976.

The organic architecture of Porto Cervo, 1960s.

Left: Local flora of Costa Smeralda.

Right: Veronica Pasini photographed by Ina Cenusa in front of Stella Maris Church.

Costa Smeralda offers ideal winds for thrilling regattas.

Verdant path leading to the beach.

The Meyers Manx and Fiat's Spiaggina are the preferred mode of transportation in Costa Smeralda.

Left: Sign along the Pevero Health Trail pointing to the many wonders of Costa Smeralda.

Right: The Pevero Health Trail extends for some 13 kilometers through the areas of Pevero and Romazzino.

Yellow gorse blooming in springtime.

Cala Liccia, one of the many coves along the coast.

Wildlife on the rocky coastline.

Left: The scents of cistus, myrtle, mastic, olive, strawberry, heather and juniper abound in Costa Smeralda.

Right: Hotel Cala di Volpe's electric Fiat 500 Spiaggina, eco-friendly and chic.

Undulating coastline of the Cervo Hotel beach.

Spiaggia del Principe, near Cala di Volpe, is an oasis of serenity.

Elephant Rock at Spiaggia dell'Elefante, near Cala di Volpe.

Left: Underwater adventures, photographed by Sardinian local Marcello Chiodino.

Right: Crystalline waters of Costa Smeralda.

Surrounded by juniper trees, Grande Pevero Beach is beloved by guests.

Barbara Selvaggia Borromeo wades in the transparent waters of Costa Smeralda, photographed by Slim Aarons, 1967.

A cloudless day at Spiaggia del Principe.

Model Veruschka takes a dip in the Tyrrhenian Sea, 1964. Photographed by Johnny Moncada.

Left: Rose cistus on pink granite rocks.

Right: Jetty at Hotel Cala di Volpe.

Roger Moore stars as James Bond in *The Spy Who Loved Me* (1977), filmed in Porto Cervo.

Capo Ferro lighthouse, built in 1858.

Left: *Costa Smeralda*, by Marco Glaviano, 2005.

Right: Olimpia Hruska poses against a rock in Costa Smeralda. Photographed by Slim Aarons, 1964.

Left: The 363rd edition of the Festival of Sant'Efisio, 2019. A procession of the statue of the patron saint of Cagliari and Sardinia is accompanied by a crowd dressed in traditional costumes.

Right: Hotel Cala di Volpe.

Left: Stella Maris Church, designed by architect Michele Busiri-Vici.

Right: Traditional religious ceremonies in Sardinia.

Fishermen on Sardinia's Emerald Coast in the 1960s.

Calm waters of Sardinia at dawn.

Left: Mural in the village of San Sperate, in southern Sardinia.

Right: *Orriu* manufacturer, mats made by weaving cane, in Milis, near the western coast of Sardinia. Photographed by Mario de Biasi, 1955.

Dolores Guinness in Porto Cervo. Photographed by Slim Aarons, 1965.

Mixed stones and pastel colors adorn the buildings of Cala di Volpe.

Exploring the diverse Sardinian landscape.

The beautiful village of Porto Cervo is the heart of Costa Smeralda.

Bagaglino neighborhood near Liscia di Vacca Bay.

Left: Picturesque view from a suite at Hotel Cala di Volpe.

Right: The façades of Hotel Cala di Volpe mirror the landscape's spring palette.

Left: Villa Anthas at Hotel Pitrizza is seamlessly integrated into its lush surroundings.

Right: Designer Sara Melis and Guglielmo Miani, CEO of Larusmiani, lounge in the Mediterranean sun.

The seaside villas of Hotel Pitrizza feature private pools.

Casa di Sopra, the presidential suite at Hotel Pitrizza.

The Sculpture House by architect Jacques Couëlle, 1962. Sinuous forms became a quintessential element in Couëlle's designs for Costa Smeralda.

Bettina Graziani relaxes in Costa Smeralda. Photographed by Slim Aarons, 1964.

Hotel Pitrizza, located among the rocks and flowers.

Villa designed by Jacques Couëlle, overlooking Cala di Volpe.

Jacques Couëlle helped define the architectural style of Costa Smeralda, combining curved lines and the raw elements of the landscape.

The façade of Jacques Couëlle's organically shaped structure is embellished with a blue-green mosaic, mirroring the colors of the bay.

Nuraghi, ancient megalithic edifices, are found exclusively on Sardinia, in Arzachena.

Paola d'Assche and Margherita Stabiumi in Costa Smeralda.

Villa Corbezzolo at Hotel Pitrizza.

Modern, natural interior designed by Savin Couëlle.

Left: Organically carved staircase by Savin Couëlle.

Right: The white-hued interiors by Savin Couëlle complement the emerald tones of Costa Smeralda's landscape.

Villa dei Due Mari (House of Two Seas), by architect Savin Couëlle, in Sardinia.

Left: Guglielmo Miani has been visiting Costa Smeralda since he was born and recently decided to relocate to Porto Cervo.

Right: Hotel Cala di Volpe, 1960s.

Left: Henry Bentivoglio Middleton and his wife dock their yacht *Miss Two* at the Porto Cervo harbor, 1978. Photographed by Slim Aarons.

Right: The Guinness family sailing off Costa Smeralda. Photographed by Slim Aarons, 1967.

Fleet race during the 2007 Maxi Yacht Rolex Cup, an event held annually in the waters of Costa Smeralda.

Victoria Beckham enjoys a boat ride off the coast of Sardinia.

Left: Relaxing on the waves of the Tyrrhenian Sea.

Right: Boat with a spinnaker off Costa Smeralda, 1973. Photographed by Slim Aarons.

Magic Carpet during the 2007 Maxi Yacht Rolex Cup.

Left: The latest fashions of Costa Smeralda, illustrated by Poppy Waddilove.

Right: Yacht guests, including Aga Khan and actor Peter Sellers, in Costa Smeralda, 1967. Photographed by Slim Aarons.

Sailing yachts adorned in *gran pavese*, a series of ceremonial flags, and moored in Porto Cervo, 1960s.

Grace Kelly strolls along the harbor of Costa Smeralda.

Luxury cars and impressive yachts line the harbors of Costa Smeralda.

Prince Karim Aga Khan with a model of Porto Cervo. He closely oversaw the development of Costa Smeralda, creating the exclusive destination it is today. Photographed by Slim Aarons, 1960.

The lively Porto Cervo Marina.

Promenade du Port, the cultural hub of Porto Cervo, with galleries, restaurants and concept stores.

Claudia Schiffer takes advantage of Costa Smeralda's pristine beaches.

Left: Stunning views of the bay accompany every visit to the Atrium Bar at Hotel Cala di Volpe.

Right: The quaint Porto Cervo Marina at the time of Costa Smeralda's development.

The grand terrace of the Royal Suite at Cervo Hotel.

Left: Encounters at the Kabouga Club di Sa Conca, 1960s.

Right: Colorful stairs accent the white architecture and wooden details in a suite at Hotel Cala di Volpe.

Stone architecture is the preferred building style in Costa Smeralda.

Left: Quite corner at Cala di Volpe.

Right: Stairs in Porto Cervo mimicking the organic curves of the surrounding nature.

Left: Minimalist corridors in Cala di Volpe.

Right: Handprints on the archway add a whimsical touch to this Cala di Volpe staircase.

Left: The ideal outdoor space, overlooking Cala Monti Zoppu.

Right: Illustration of Costa Smeralda by Poppy Waddilove.

Left: Marisa Berenson photographed by Henry Clarke for *Vogue*, 1969.

Right: Vibrant entrance to a suite at Hotel Cala di Volpe.

Left: Hotel Cala di Volpe weaves together the natural elements of Costa Smeralda with the modern architecture.

Right: Interplay of shadows at Hotel Cala di Volpe.

Stained-glass details accent the white stucco of Hotel Cala di Volpe.

Left: Picturesque seating area at Hotel Cala di Volpe.

Right: Illustration by Poppy Waddilove capturing la dolce vita of Costa Smeralda.

Left: Dolce&Gabbana seasonal pop-up shop in Hotel Cala di Volpe.

Right: Costa Smeralda scenes, illustrated by Poppy Waddilove.

The Tree of Life, a temporary mural on the stairs of the Church of Santa Lucia in Arzachena by Giorgio Casu.

Left: Cerasarda is a brand synonymous with the ceramics of Costa Smeralda.

Right: The Cerasarda ceramics factory originated in 1963 at the request of Aga Khan.

Left: Handmade process of decorating Cerasarda ceramics.

Right: Ceramic fish handcrafted in Sardinia by Artigianato Pasella.

Simone D'Aillencourt, wearing Emilio Pucci, at Hotel Cala di Volpe. Photographed by Henry Clarke for *Vogue*, 1967.

The reception area at Hotel Cala di Volpe extends an elevated yet bohemian welcome.

Left: Entrepreneur Aureta Thomollari selects a mini convertible as her Sardinian transportation of choice.

Right: Jacopo Signani and Guglielmo Miani, both wearing Larusmiani, in Porto Cervo.

Left: Private cabanas at Nikki Beach Costa Smeralda.

Right: Photo shoot at Hotel Cala di Volpe, 1960s.

Nikki Beach restaurant on Cala Petra Ruja.

Left: Restaurants in Costa Smeralda have been offering the finest cuisine and bringing people together for decades.

Right: Delectable dishes of fresh ingredients served beachside at Cala Beach Club.

Left: Finishing touches for the Gala Dinner at Hotel Romazzino.

Right: Alfresco dining at Cala di Volpe Barbecue.

Left: Beefbar at Hotel Cala di Volpe.

Right: Private wine cellar in the Harrods Suite of Hotel Cala di Volpe.

Hotel Cala di Volpe's newly renovated Lobby Bar.

Left: Tanning on the sands of Spiaggia del Principe.

Right: A coconut refreshment at Cala Beach Club.

Exclusive lounge area at Cala Beach Club.

Hotel Pitrizza, a Mediterranean oasis of luxury and serenity.

Left: Crystal-clear waters are characteristic of Costa Smeralda's beaches.

Right: Private swimming pool at Hotel Cala di Volpe's Harrods Suite.

White architectural details at Hotel Romazzino's Villa Smeralda.

Left: Costa Smeralda is a tranquil escape where visitors can relax and indulge.

Right: Stella Maris Church, a cultural treasure in the Gulf of Porto Cervo, features a conical bell tower.

Footpath through the blossoming Mediterranean maquis of Costa Smeralda.

Left: The course at Pevero Golf Club was designed by Robert Trent Jones.

Right: Robert Trent Jones's daring design stretches through rocky terrain and flora.

A round of golf at Pevero Golf Club, 1970s.

The Pevero Golf Club estate extends from the Gulf of Pevero to Cala di Volpe.

Left: Guests participate in a game of padel at Cervo Hotel.

Right: Tennis court surrounded by greenery at Hotel Romazzino.

Hotel Romazzino offers a range of water sports for adventure seekers and beachgoers.

Left: Waterskiing in front of Hotel Pitrizza, 1970s.

Right: Barbara Selvaggia Borromeo on holiday in Costa Smeralda, 1967. Photographed by Slim Aarons.

Sailing yacht on the majestic waters of Costa Smeralda.

An impressive fleet of yachts at Porto Cervo.

Private aircrafts carry the jet set to and from the chic destination of Costa Smeralda.

The magical Hotel Cala di Volpe at dusk.

Revelers enjoy the pleasant evening climate of Costa Smeralda.

The lively Gala Dinner hosted at Hotel Cala di Volpe.

The swimming pool of the Harrods Suite features a built-in bar with an incomparable view.

Left: In Costa Smeralda, the fun continues after the sun sets.

Right: The legendary Beefbar restaurant.

Tables are set for dinner at
Romazzino Barbecue.

The annual summer pop-up
village, Waterfront, animates
the evenings at Porto Cervo.

Yacht Club Costa Smeralda,
established by the Aga Khan,
André Ardoin, Giuseppe
Mentasti and Luigi Vietti
in 1967, at Porto Cervo.

Quiet moment spent on a
Costa Smeralda beach.

Left: Couple posing with a Fiat 125
on Liscia di Vacca Beach, 1967.

Right: Costa Smeralda's bustling
nightlife with VIPs such as
Princess Caroline of Monaco,
Flavio Briatore, Vanessa Hudgens,
Mohammed Al Turki, Simona
Molinari and Jasmine Tookes.

Dinner with a view at Porto Cervo.

Breathtaking, golden sunset.

Left: Elegant guest attends "L'Art de
Vivre a Porto Cervo" private party
at Pedrinelli Restaurant, 2018.

Right: Full moon over the
Liscia Ruja Beach.

Hotel Cala di Volpe's Gala Dinner,
"Something Blue," organized
by Filmmaster Events.

Liscia Ruja cove dotted
with yachts.

ACKNOWLEDGMENTS

Special thanks to Qatar Investment Authority, Consorzio Costa Smeralda, Smeralda Holding, Mario Ferraro, Antonella Azara, and Maurizio Maresca.

The publisher would like to thank the following: Mary Ellen Jensen, Alamy Stock Photo; Leslie Amon; Archivio Ilisso Edizioni; Artigianato Pasella; Marisa Berenson; Carlo Borlenghi; Davide Caglio; Antonio Cesari; Paola d' Assche; Piotr Degler, Degler Studio; Mara Mibelli, Engel & Völkers Porto Cervo; Vincenzo Frigo; Anthony Tran, Gallery Stock; Brian Stehlin, Getty Images; Gruppo Editoriale; Gruppo Romani; Ted Gushue; Roberto Rossi Gandolfi, Handbook; Valentina Moncada, Johnny Moncada Archive; Guglielmo Miani, Solange Zurcher, Larusmiani; Andrea Luzardi; Francesca Turrin, Marco Glaviano; Emanuelet Massolini; Federica Fiorenza, Maritza Solorzano, Nikki Beach Costa Smeralda; Guido Piga; PSE Editore; Daniel Rodriguez, Redux Pictures; Vincent Mounier, Shutterstock; Sonia Ricour-Lambard, SO Represent; Marina Camargo, Nik Neves, Wonderful World of Maps.

CREDITS

Pp. 4-5: © Jean-Pierre Degas/Hemis/Alamy Stock Photo; pp. 6-7, 10-11, 54, 55, 58-59, 64-67, 69, 70, 72-73, 84-85, 90, 128-129, 162-165, 192, 227-229, 231, 234-235, 242-243, 260-261, 264-265, 270-271: © Marcello Chiodino; pp. 8, 14-15, 141, 156, 172, 205, 208, 232-233, 240, 250-251, 256: © Nello Di Salvo @ coastmagazine; p. 17: Artwork by Josh McKenna; pp. 20, 182, 198-199: © Henry Clarke/Condé Nast/Shutterstock; pp. 21, 48-49, 60-62, 71, 76-77, 80, 222, 252-253, 273, 276-277: Photo by Paolo Curto/Courtesy of Smeralda Holding Archive; pp. 24-25, 40-41, 44-45, 91 (bottom left), 92-93, 154-155, 169, 174, 177: Courtesy of Consorzio Costa Smeralda; pp. 27, 52-53: © Piotr Degler/Degler Studio; pp. 30-31, 74-75, 87, 118-119, 142, 143, 149, 153, 160-161, 241: © Slim Aarons/Hulton Archive/Getty Images; pp. 34-35, 81, 108, 112-113, 120-121, 170-171, 176, 179, 187, 190, 200-201, 209, 210, 214-215, 217-221, 236-239, 258-259, 274-275: Photo by White Box Studio/Courtesy of Smeralda Holding Archive; pp. 36-37, 46, 89, 101, 168, 173, 178, 184, 185, 211-213, 223, 254-255, 257: © Andrea Garuti; p. 38: Photo by Dario Garofalo for *Cosmho*/Courtesy Gruppo Editoriale S.r.l.; p. 39: © Kos Picture Source/Getty Images; p. 42: © Patrick Lichfield/Condé Nast/Shutterstock; pp. 43, 98-99: © Slim Aarons/Getty Images; p. 47: Photographer: Ina Cenusa/Model: Veronica Pasini, Iso Model Management; pp. 50-51: Courtesy of Davide Caglio Photography; p. 57: © Antonella Azara; p. 63: © Emanuele Massolini; p. 79: Courtesy of Johnny Moncada Archive; pp. 82-83: © Danjaq/EON/UA Britain/Kobal/Shutterstock; p. 86: © Marco Glaviano; p. 88: © Jean-Michel Roignant/Andia/Universal Images Group/Getty Images; p. 91 (top left, bottom right): © Stefania Porcu/Gallery Stock; p. 91 (top right): © Emanuele Perrone; pp. 94-95: © Patrizio Martorana/Dreamstime; p. 96: Photo by Vincenzo Frigo/Courtesy of *Costa Smeralda Magazine*/PSE Editore Archives; p. 97: Milis, 1955-58, Mario De Biasi/Archivio Ilisso Edizioni; pp. 102-103: © Stefano Oppo/Getty Images; p. 105: © Milena Boeva/Alamy Stock Photo; pp. 106-107: © Massimo Piacentino/Alamy Stock Photo; pp. 109, 110, 114-115, 132-133, 224, 230, 248-249: Photo by Tiziano Canu/Courtesy of Smeralda Holding Archive; pp. 111, 203: © Andrea Luzardi; pp. 116-117: © Christophe Coënon/*AD* Magazine; pp. 122-127: Photo by Gianluca Muscas/Courtesy of Engel & Völkers Porto Cervo; p. 131: Courtesy of Paola d' Assche; pp. 134-137, 139: © Tiziano Canu; pp. 140, 202: © Ted Gushue; pp. 144-145, 150-151: © Carlo Borlenghi/Icon Sportswire/Getty Images; pp. 146-147, 167: © Archivio Costa Smeralda Frezza/La Fata; p. 148: © Ashley Camper; pp. 152, 181, 189, 191: Illustration by Poppy Waddilove; pp. 158-159, 188, 268-269: © Toni Anzenberger/Redux; p. 180: © Larusmiani; p. 183: © Leslie Amon; pp. 194-196: Courtesy of Cerasarda, La ceramica della Costa Smeralda/Gruppo Romani Spa; p. 197: Courtesy of Artigianato Pasella; pp. 204, 206-207: Courtesy of Nikki Beach Costa Smeralda; p. 216: © Yadid Levy/Redux; p. 226: © Sergio del Grande/Mondadori/Getty Images; pp. 244-245: © Benoît Gysembergh *Paris Match*/Getty Images; pp. 246-247: © Antonio Cesari; pp. 262-263: © Carlo Borlenghi; p. 266: © Giorgio Lotti/Mondadori/Getty Images; p. 267, left to right, by row: (first row) Photo by Tiziano Canu/Courtesy of Smeralda Holding Archive; © Anthony Ghnassia/Getty Images for UNICEF; Photo by Tiziano Canu/Courtesy of Smeralda Holding Archive; © Archivio Costa Smeralda Frezza/La Fata; (second row) Courtesy of Davide Caglio Photography; © Nello Di Salvo @ coastmagazine; © Sunset Boulevard/Corbis/Getty Images; (third row) © Jacopo M. Raule/Getty Images for UNICEF; © Archivio Costa Smeralda Frezza/La Fata; Courtesy of Paola d' Assche; (fourth row) © Nello Di Salvo @ coastmagazine; Photo by Tiziano Canu/Courtesy of Smeralda Holding Archive; © Jacopo M. Raule/Getty Images for Luisaviaroma; p. 272: © Daniele Venturelli/Getty Images for De GRISOGONO; p. 286: © Nik Neves/Wonderful World of Maps.

Every possible effort has been made to identify and contact all rights holders and obtain their permission for work appearing in these pages. Any errors or omissions brought to the publisher's attention will be corrected in future editions.

Assouline supports *One Tree Planted*
in its commitment to create a more
sustainable world through reforestation.

Front cover design © Assouline Publishing.
Back cover tip-on (clockwise from top left):
© Marcello Chiodino; © Henry Clarke/
Condé Nast/Shutterstock; © Marcello Chiodino;
© Nello Di Salvo @ coastmagazine.
Endpages: © Nik Neves/Wonderful World of Maps.

© 2022 Assouline Publishing
A Travel From Home™ Book
3 Park Avenue, 27th floor
New York, NY 10016 USA
Tel: 212-989-6769 Fax: 212-647-0005
assouline.com

Text translated from the Italian by Luisa Nitrato Izzo.
Printed in Italy by Grafiche Milani, on Fedrigoni Symbol
Freelife paper, produced in Italy under the strictest
environmental standards.
ISBN: 9781649801005

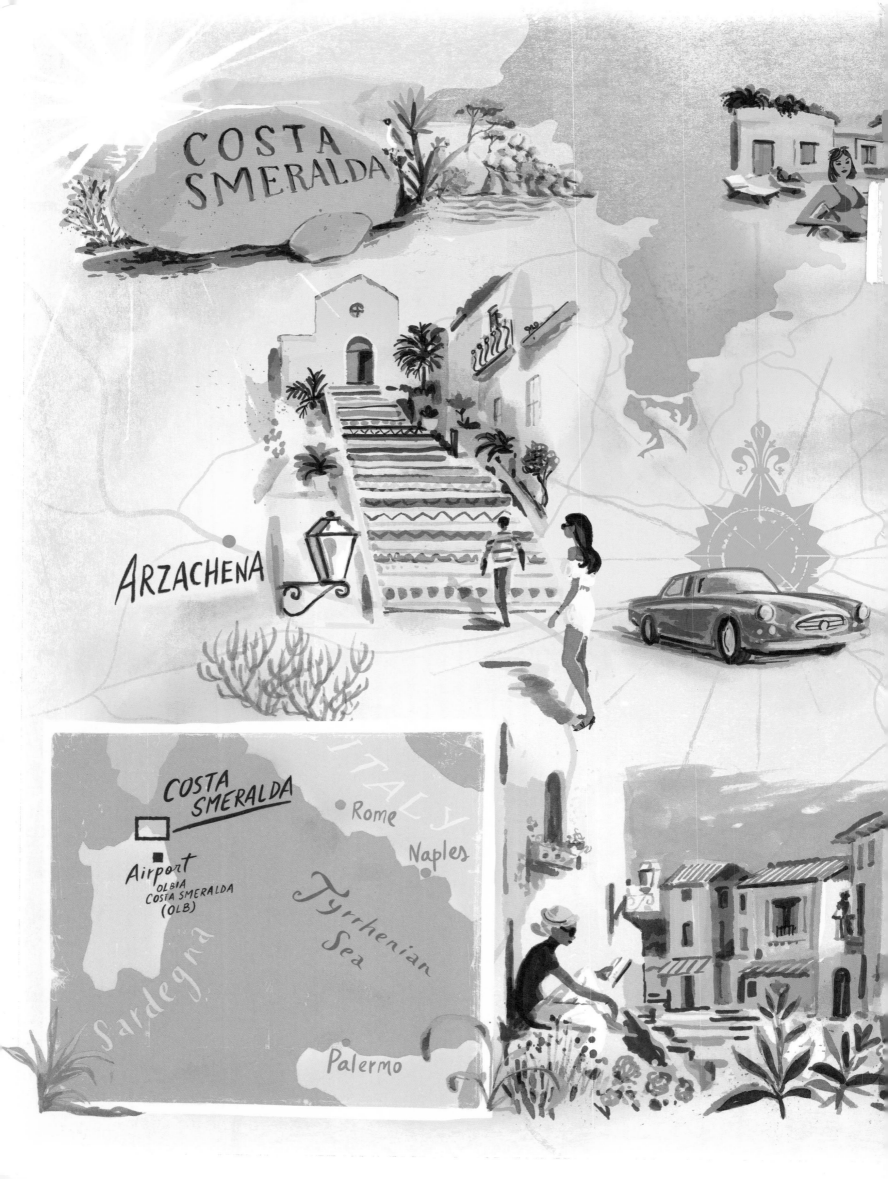